GRASSLAND FOOD CHAINS

Buffy Silverman

Chicago, Illinois

www.heinemannraintree.com
Visit our website to find out more information about Heinemann-Raintree books.

To order:

☏ Phone 888-454-2279

▭ Visit www.heinemannraintree.com to browse our catalog and order online.

Edited by Abby Colich and Andrew Farrow
Designed by Victoria Allen
Illustrated by Words and Publications
Picture research by Mica Brancic
Originated by Capstone Global Library, Ltd.
Printed by China Translation & Printing Services, Ltd.

14
10 9 8 7 6 5 4 3

Library of Congress Cataloging-in-Publication Data
Silverman, Buffy.
  Grassland food chains / Buffy Silverman.
    p. cm. -- (Protecting food chains)
  Includes bibliographical references and index.
  ISBN 978-1-4329-3857-4 (hc) -- ISBN 978-1-4329-3864-2
(pb) 1. Grassland ecology--Juvenile literature. 2. Food chains
(Ecology)--Juvenile literature. I. Title.
  QH541.5.P7S55 2011
  577.4'16--dc22
                          2009049542

Acknowledgments
Alamy p. 40 (©Michael Snel); Corbis pp. 29 (©Darrell Gulin), 43 (©Dan Guravich); Getty Images p. 8 (Tips Italia/Guido Alberto Rossi); Nature Picture Library pp. 31 (©Gertrud & Helmut Denzau), 33 (©Luiz Claudio Marigo); Photolibrary pp. 4 (Japan Travel Bureau/JTB Photo), 9 (Animals Animals/S Michael Bisceglie), 13 (Oxford Scientific (OSF)/Ariadne Van Zandbergen), 17 (age fotostock/Bruno Morandi), 18 (Juniors Bildarchiv), 19 (imagebroker.net/jspix jspix), 21 (All Canada Photos/Roberta Olenick), 22 (Animals Animals/Joe McDonald), 23 (Flirt Collection/Jeff Vanuga), 25 (age fotostock/Roger Wilmshurst), 27 (age fotostock/Jon Diez Beldarrain), 26 (imagebroker.net/Alessandra Sarti), 34 (age fotostock/Javier Larrea), 35 (Animals Animals/Doug Wechsler), 36 (Oxford Scientific (OSF)/Mark Jones), 37 (Jacques Jangoux), 39 (age fotostock/Jack Milchanowski), 41 (Animals Animals/Werner Bollmann), 42 (age fotostock/Dhritiman Mukherjee); Photoshot 38; Shutterstock pp. 15 (Manamana), 14 (Mel Brackstone).

Cover photograph of a black-tailed prairie dog reproduced with permission of Photolibrary (White).

Cover and spread background image reproduced with permission of Shutterstock (©Iakov Kalinin).

We would like to thank Kenneth Dunton and Dana Sjostrom for their invaluable help in the preparation of this book.

CONTENTS

Some words are shown in bold, **like this**. You can find out what they mean by looking in the glossary.

WHAT IS A GRASSLAND FOOD CHAIN?

On an African **savanna**, zebras **graze** on grasses. A lion creeps closer, hidden in the dry grass. The lion charges, capturing a zebra. Lions, zebras, and grass are part of a grassland food chain.

All living things need **energy** to live and grow. They get energy from food. Plants and animals that live in the same **habitat** are connected to one another by the flow of energy.

The energy in food chains begins with the Sun. Green plants use the Sun's energy to make food through a process called **photosynthesis**.

Many animals get energy and **nutrients** by eating plants. Animals use that energy to move, sleep, grow, and live. Other animals hunt for food. Their energy and nutrients come from their **prey**.

This lion is getting ready to attack zebras in a savanna in Tanzania.

When plants and animals die, their bodies still contain energy and nutrients. **Bacteria** and **fungi** break down dead **organisms**. This energy is returned to the soil, where it is used by plants. The cycle begins again.

READING A FOOD CHAIN

A food chain diagram shows how living organisms are linked together. The arrows that connect members of a food chain show how energy flows from an organism to the organism that consumes it.

If something happens to one link of a food chain, it affects the other living things in the chain. Humans are also affected when links are broken in grassland food chains. Although we have done many things to harm them, we can take steps to protect them from more damage.

This is a diagram of a grassland food chain. The arrows show how each member of the chain gets its energy.

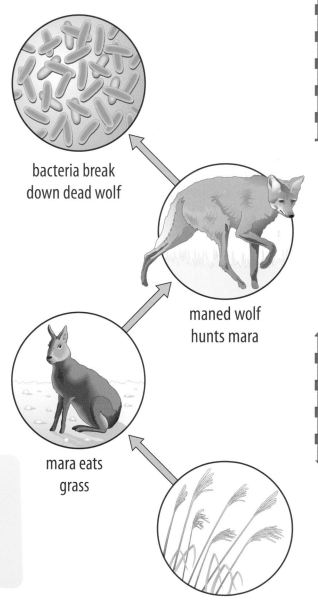

bacteria break down dead wolf

maned wolf hunts mara

mara eats grass

pampas grass

WHAT ARE THE PARTS OF A FOOD CHAIN?

A food chain links three or more organisms in a habitat: a **producer**, a **consumer**, and a **decomposer**. Plants are producers. They use the Sun's energy to make food in a process called photosynthesis. Plants are at the start of a food chain.

The next link in a food chain is an animal that eats a producer. It might be a monarch butterfly that sips flower **nectar**, a bird that eats seeds, or a grasshopper that chews grass. All of these animals are **primary consumers**. They get energy by consuming producers. They are **herbivores**, or animals that eat plants.

Animals that eat other animals are called **secondary consumers**. They are **carnivores**, which means that they eat meat. A bluebird that eats grasshoppers is a secondary consumer. It might be the next link in a food chain.

All living organisms die. Decomposers are organisms that break down dead plants and animals. They return nutrients to the food chain.

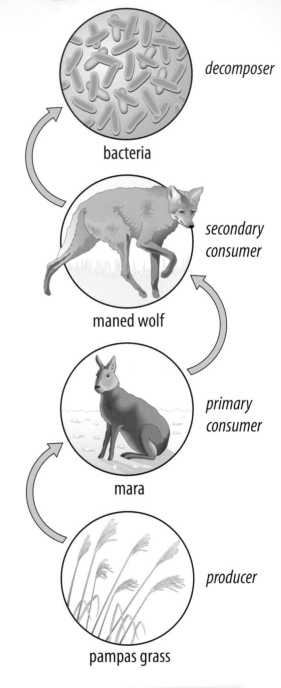

decomposer

bacteria

secondary consumer

maned wolf

primary consumer

mara

producer

pampas grass

This food chain shows how energy flows from producer (**pampas** grass) to decomposer (bacteria).

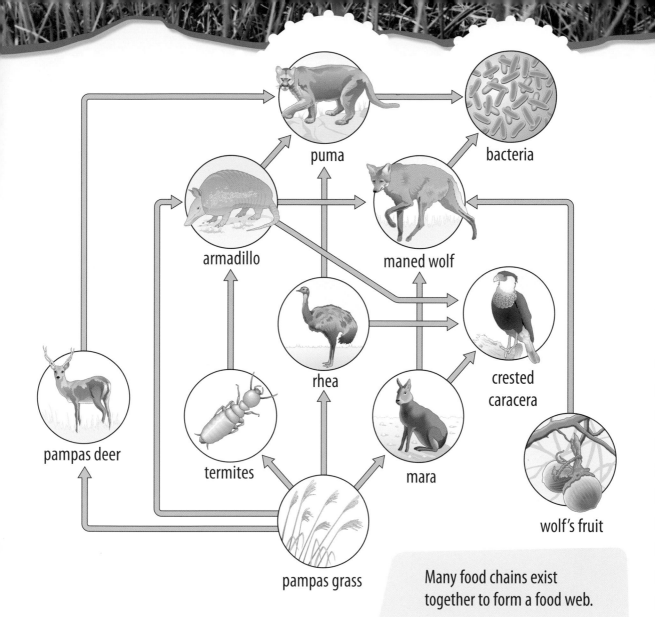

puma

bacteria

armadillo

maned wolf

rhea

crested
caracera

pampas deer

termites

mara

wolf's fruit

pampas grass

Many food chains exist
together to form a food web.

WHAT IS A FOOD WEB?

Different food chains in the same habitat can be connected as a food
web. A food chain follows a single path, showing the flow of energy
and nutrients along that chain. But in nature, many organisms eat the
same food. A food web is made of several food chains linked together.
It shows the different paths energy and nutrients can travel.

The arrows in a food web show the flow of energy and nutrients
from producers to primary consumers, to secondary consumers,
and to decomposers. The arrows lead from plants, to animals that
eat plants, to animals that eat animals.

WHAT IS A GRASSLAND HABITAT?

What grows in a grassland? Grass! There are two main types of grasslands in the world. Grasslands in **tropical** regions are warm all year long. Grasslands in **temperate** regions have hot summers and cold winters. There may even be grasslands such as meadows in your local area.

In the tropics, grasslands are called **savannas**. Tropical grasslands grow in Africa, Australia, South America, and India. If you look out on a savanna, you see scattered trees surrounded by grasses. All savannas have a wet season followed by a dry season. The rainy season lasts from six to eight months. During the dry season, little rain falls and fires are common. Plants that thrive on a savanna are **adapted** to survive fire and drought. Without these conditions, trees would sprout and the savanna would change into a forest.

A huge variety of grasses, shrubs, and other plants grow on savannas. They provide insects, reptiles, birds, and **mammals** with food and homes.

Wildebeests are adapted to living in a grassland **habitat**.

Bison live and graze on the North American prairie.

TALL AND SHORT GRASSLANDS

Temperate grasslands are given different names in different places. North American **prairies**, Russian **steppes**, South African **velds**, and South American **pampas** are all grasslands. The type of grass that grows depends on the amount of rainfall. A temperate grassland receives between 50 and 90 centimeters (20 and 35 inches) of rain a year. Tall grass grows where there is more rain. With less rain, shorter grasses grow.

The soils of temperate grasslands are richer than those in the tropics. Temperate grasslands have deep, dark soils. Because they are flat and have rich soils, many temperate grasslands have been turned into farms and **grazing** lands.

' 'HERE IN THE ' 'ORLD ARE GRASSLAND HABITATS?

This map shows some of the world's major grassland **habitats**.

NORTH
AMERICA

North American prairies

desert grasslands

SOUTH
AMERICA

South American pampas

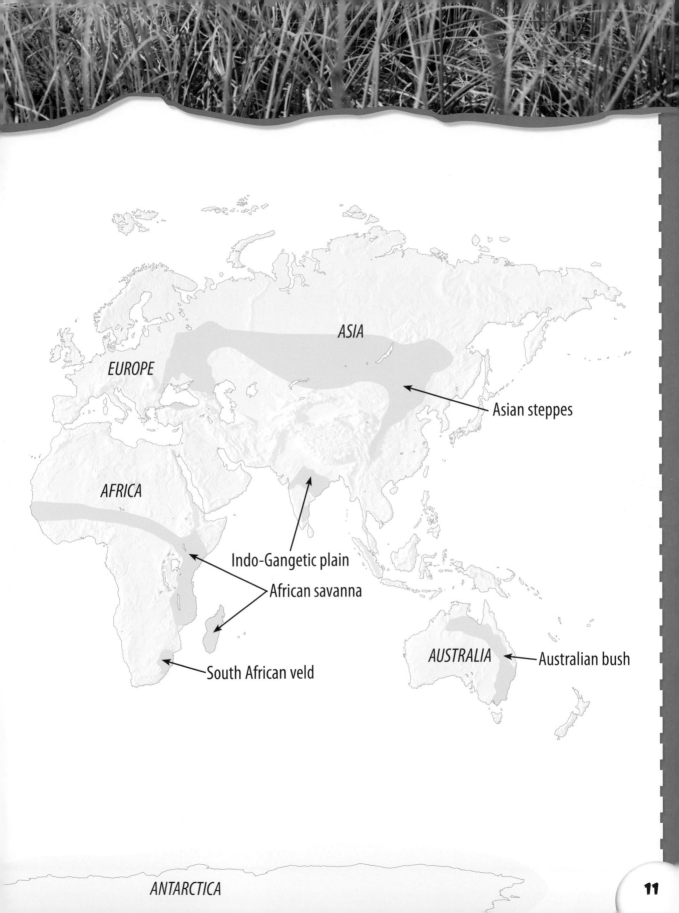

EUROPE

ASIA

Asian steppes

AFRICA

Indo-Gangetic plain

African savanna

South African veld

AUSTRALIA Australian bush

ANTARCTICA

WHAT ARE THE PRODUCERS IN GRASSLANDS?

The most common **producer** in any grassland **habitat** is grass. Like all producers, grasses use the Sun's **energy** to produce food in their long, narrow leaves. The food that they make fuels their growth. **Nutrients** and energy move along the food chain to animals that **graze** on grasses.

Although all grasslands have grasses, they do not have the same types of grasses. The type of grass that grows depends on **climate**, rainfall, and soil. With plenty of rainfall, tall, thick grasses grow, such as **pampas** grass in Argentina. During the warm, humid summers, dense stands of grasses shoot up. With few trees to shade them, grasses get plenty of sunlight and grow quickly. The wind blows clouds of **pollen** from one plant to another. After a grass plant is **pollinated**, it makes many seeds. Wind and animals carry the seeds, spreading grass plants to new places. Wildflowers also grow among grasses.

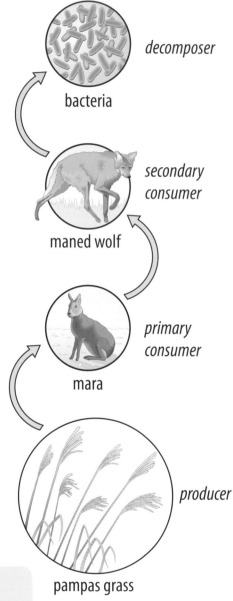

decomposer

bacteria

secondary consumer

maned wolf

primary consumer

mara

producer

pampas grass

Producers such as grasses are at the start of grassland food chains. They produce food in their leaves.

Rheas search for grass seeds to eat. They scatter some seeds when walking through grasses, planting new plants.

Why do grasses grow in so many places? Grasses are **adapted** to grow even when water is scarce. One example is grasses with narrow leaves, from which less water **evaporates** than on plants with wide leaves. Grasses grow thick mats of roots below ground. During a drought, they reach water far below the surface. Some grasses are curved to collect and funnel water toward their roots.

In places where less rain falls, grasses do not grow as tall or as thick. Regions that are covered with short grasses are called **steppes**. The soils are not as deep or rich on a steppe. Summers in the steppe are hot and dry, and winters are very cold. The grasses that grow here survive drought, fire, and windstorms.

WHERE ARE THE TREES?

Trees grow along rivers and streams in a **temperate** grassland. In the vast fields, there is too little rain for trees to thrive.

Grass plants spread from stems growing below and above ground. Stems that creep below ground are called **rhizomes**. Dense roots grow down from rhizomes. This solid mat of roots leaves little space for tree seedlings to sprout. Stems that spread on the surface are called **stolons**. Shoots of grasses grow up from rhizomes and stolons.

During summer droughts, fires started by lightning are common. Winds spread fires, killing tree seedlings. But grasses are adapted to survive. Much of a grass plant is safe below ground and will grow new shoots after a fire. After animals graze on grasses, they also send up new shoots.

After a fire, grasses grow quickly from underground roots.

SAVANNAS

On a **tropical savanna**, clumps of trees are scattered among grasses. These trees must go many months without water.

Baobab trees grow in African and Australian savannas. A baobab's long **taproot** reaches far below ground to get water. During the rainy season, a baobab tree can store 120,000 liters (32,000 gallons) of water in its huge trunk. It uses the water to survive the dry season. The tree also sheds leaves during droughts. Without leaves, it does not lose water. The tree's thick bark protects it from wildfires.

Overgrazing by cattle harms **native** grasses. Animals that depend on grasses have trouble finding enough to eat.

LOSING A LINK: BUNCHGRASSES

Bunchgrasses are native to grasslands of the southwestern United States. They are a favorite food for insects, birds, and **mammals**. But bunchgrasses are becoming rare. Since the late 1800s, ranchers have brought cattle to graze. The cattle **overgraze** and kill bunchgrasses. Many of the **primary consumers** that depend on bunchgrasses are becoming **extinct**.

WHAT ARE THE PRIMARY CONSUMERS IN GRASSLANDS?

Energy and **nutrients** flow from plants to **primary consumers** in a grassland food chain. Many **consumers** eat grassland plants. Insects such as grasshoppers and beetles have strong jaws for chewing tough grass. Bees, butterflies, birds, and bats sip **nectar** and eat **pollen** from flowers. Grassland birds eat seeds. Large animals **graze** on grasses and eat tree leaves.

TUNNELING BELOW

Mice, voles, moles, and other rodents burrow through soil in grasslands. They find and eat roots and **tubers**. At night some rodents go above ground and eat seeds and green parts of plants. By tunneling through soil, they mix around nutrients, improving the soil. They also spread seeds so new plants can grow.

Plains pocket gophers are rodents that live on **prairies**. They spend almost their entire lives underground, gnawing on roots and tubers. Their large front feet have strong claws for digging burrows. Pocket gophers avoid many **predators** by living below ground. If a predator digs below ground, a pocket gopher can run backward as fast as it runs forward. It uses its tail to feel its way.

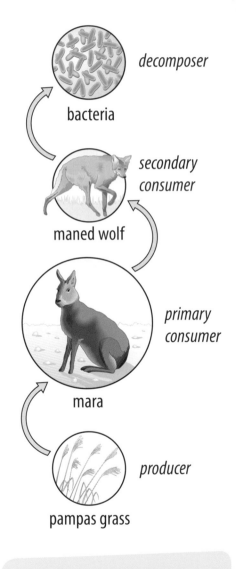

decomposer

bacteria

secondary consumer

maned wolf

primary consumer

mara

producer

pampas grass

Primary consumers such as the mara eat **producers** such as **pampas** grasses.

The number of wild horses on the Mongolian steppe has shrunk drastically.

GRAZERS

Large animals that eat grasses and other plants are called **grazers**. On an open field, predators can easily spot their **prey**. Antelopes and other grazing animals have long legs and hoofs to help them outrun predators.

Today, there are fewer animals grazing on grasslands. Farming and ranching have changed their **habitats**. Hunting has also taken a toll on their numbers. Thousands of wild horses, called Przewalski's horses, once lived on the Mongolian **steppe**. Between 300 and 400 Przewalski's horses now live in the wild.

Zebra and wildebeest graze together on African savannas.

TROPICAL GRASSLANDS

Grazing animals must **adapt** to a changing food and water supply on **tropical savannas**. During the wet season, trees are covered with leaves, and lush grasses grow. After the rains end, water holes dry out. Many trees drop their leaves, and grasses die. Some primary consumers **migrate** to find food and water. Others can survive for months without drinking.

In the evening and at night, red kangaroos graze on grasses and other plants in Australian grasslands. During the day, they sleep under shady bushes. Kangaroos usually stay in small groups of about 10. Occasionally 1,000 kangaroos or more will come together when they find a good food source.

On African savannas, herds of ostrich, zebra, wildebeest, and antelope travel and graze together. Different animals eat different parts of plants, so they do not compete for food. When grasses grow thickly, zebras eat and trample taller plants. That exposes shorter grasses, which wildebeest prefer. Wildebeest and zebras migrate to follow the rains. When the rainy season ends, the animals often move to grasslands that border lakes.

LOSING A LINK: AFRICAN BUSH ELEPHANT

The African bush elephant is the world's largest land animal. This 11-ton giant eats about 160 kilograms (350 pounds) of plants a day. To find enough food, elephants must range over a large area. Loss of savanna habitats puts them at risk. Elephant populations have also declined because of hunting. People hunt elephants for their ivory tusks. Due to hunting, African elephant populations almost went **extinct**. The ivory trade was banned worldwide in 1989, but some people still hunt elephants.

The population of African bush elephants is threatened by loss of habitat and hunting.

WHAT ARE THE SECONDARY CONSUMERS IN GRASSLANDS?

Secondary consumers are predators that hunt animals. Some eat both plants and animals. In a food chain, primary consumers take in energy and nutrients captured by plants. When a primary consumer is eaten, some of its energy and nutrients become part of secondary consumers.

INSECT EATERS

Huge numbers of grasshoppers, crickets, beetles, grubs, and caterpillars munch on grassland plants. These insects attract secondary consumers. Birds, snakes, spiders, turtles, lizards, and other animals feast on grassland insects.

In the summer, a bird called a bobolink nests on the ground in the grasslands of Canada and the northern United States. It searches for insects to feed its growing young. When summer ends in the northern hemisphere, bobolinks migrate. They fly to grasslands in Argentina and Brazil.

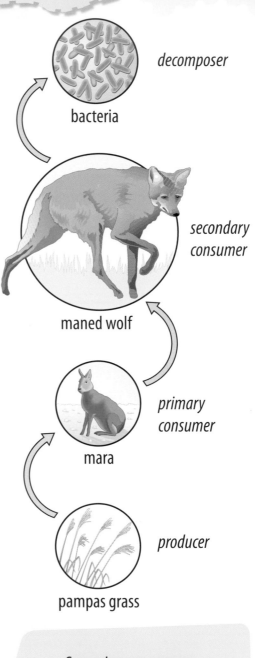

decomposer

bacteria

secondary consumer

maned wolf

primary consumer

mara

producer

pampas grass

Secondary consumers such as the maned wolf hunt animals for food.

Burrowing owls search for insects in dry grasslands.

BIRDS OF PREY

Hawks, eagles, and owls are secondary consumers in most grasslands. These **birds of prey** fly over fields, looking for **prey**. Burrowing owls live in the dry grasslands of North and South America. They hover above ground to search for insects, toads, lizards, and rodents. Instead of nesting in trees, these small owls build their nests in underground burrows.

Most birds of prey use their excellent vision to hunt from high in the sky. The secretary bird takes a different approach. It walks across grassy **savannas** in Africa on its long legs. It stomps thick tufts of grass, flushing out prey. Then the bird races after its prey and scoops it up. If a secretary bird finds a snake or other large prey, it will stamp it to death with its powerful feet. Secretary birds may walk 32 kilometers (20 miles) a day in search of insects, small **mammals** and birds, lizards, and snakes.

HUNTING REPTILES

Snakes, lizards, and turtles live in many grasslands. They bask in sunlight to warm their bodies. These grassland reptiles find many small animals to hunt in a grassland: insects, toads, lizards, rodents, and birds.

During the rainy season, savanna monitor lizards catch plenty of food. They store fat so they can survive the dry season. Monitors flick their tongues to find birds, snakes, small mammals, toads, lizards, eggs, and snails.

A monitor lizard uses its tongue to hunt animals.

PROTECTING A LINK: BLACK-FOOTED FERRET

The black-footed ferret is a secondary consumer. It lives only in North American prairies. The ferret spends most of its time underground, hunting prairie dogs. Today the black-footed ferret is one of the most **endangered** animals in the world. That is because the number of prairie dogs has dropped sharply. Farmers poisoned prairie dogs and plowed much of the prairie, destroying prairie dog towns. Without prairie dogs, the black-footed ferret could not survive. When only 18 ferrets remained in the wild, scientists caught them. After breeding them in captivity, they released the ferrets. There are now about 2,100 black-footed ferrets living in the wild.

In the wild, black-footed ferrets eat prairie dogs. When many prairie dogs were hunted, the black-footed ferret had nothing to eat.

CATS AND DOGS

Each grassland is home to a few key large predators that hunt **grazing** animals. Cheetahs sprint after gazelles in an African savanna. A pride of lions attacks a wildebeest. A silent leopard stalks an impala. A cougar ambushes a deer in a South American **pampas**. In an Australian savanna, a pack of dingoes attacks a kangaroo or wallaby. Wolf packs hunt elk in the Canadian **prairie**. These large predators hunt over large areas to find enough prey.

WHAT ARE THE DECOMPOSERS IN GRASSLANDS?

Decomposers are an important part of a grassland food chain. They break down dead plants, animals, and animal wastes to obtain **energy**. As they do this, they release **nutrients** that create a rich soil for plants.

BACTERIA AND FUNGI

Bacteria are too small to see without a microscope. Millions and millions of them grow on dead plants and animals and in the soil. They reproduce very quickly. These huge numbers of bacteria use up the matter in dead **organisms**. They recycle and release nutrients to the soil.

Fungi also help break down dead plants and animals. A mushroom is the part of a fungus that makes **spores**. Fungi reproduce by making spores that float in the air. When spores land on dead matter, they start to grow into new fungi. A fungus grows a mass of white threads through dead plants or animals.

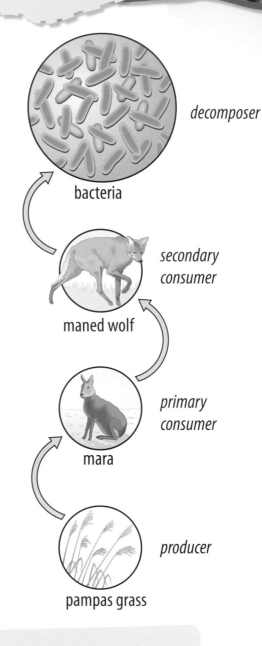

decomposer

bacteria

secondary consumer

maned wolf

primary consumer

mara

producer

pampas grass

Decomposers break down dead plants, animals, and animal wastes, releasing energy back into the food chain.

Fungi grow unseen in the soil in a grassland. Mushrooms that grow up from the underground fungi make spores.

Bacteria and fungi digest food outside of their bodies. They release chemicals called **enzymes** onto dead matter. Enzymes help break down matter into smaller compounds that can dissolve in water. Bacteria or fungi absorb these dissolved compounds and use the food energy to live and grow. Some of the dissolved nutrients become part of the soil.

In a grassland, most plants have **symbiotic** fungi growing on their roots. In a symbiotic relationship, two different **species** live together and help each other. Grassland plants gain from having fungi on their roots. The fungi let them absorb more water and nutrients from the soil. In return the plants make and give fungi sugary food. That helps the fungi grow.

In some savannas, trees grow on termite mounds. They take nutrients from plant matter that the termites break down.

GRASSLAND SCAVENGERS

Many **scavengers** live in grassland soils. They break apart plants and animals into small pieces that decomposers can break down.

Earthworms in grassland soils eat dead plant matter, breaking it into smaller pieces and mixing it in the soil. Their tunnels let air and water into soil. Earthworms help make the soil fertile, so grasses can grow.

Insects such as flies and wasps lay their eggs in dead animals in grasslands. The **larvae** that hatch then eat and break down the flesh. Burying beetles bury a mouse or bird **carcass** beneath the soil. They make a chamber inside it where the female lays her eggs. Both parents feed the larvae bits of carcass until the larvae can feed themselves.

Termites build huge mounds on the **savannas** of Australia and Africa. The termites eat dead grasses and trees such as acacia. Microscopic organisms in a termite's gut digest tough materials in grass and wood. Termites store food inside a mound, which stays cool and moist all year.

MAKING A LINK: AUSTRALIAN COW PASTURES

Dung beetles break down animal wastes. They use dung for food and lay their eggs in it. Australian dung beetles **evolved** to break down hard, fibrous kangaroo dung. When cattle were brought to Australian savannas, Australian dung beetles could not break down large, moist cow pads. The cow pads dried up, taking months to break down. Flies bred in the cow pads and bothered the cattle. The cattle would not graze on the cow pad-covered **pastures**. In the 1960s, a scientist introduced several new species of dung beetles that could break down cow dung. The dung beetles buried cow dung on Australian pastures, so it quickly disappeared.

Dung beetles roll feces (poo) into balls and then lay their eggs in them.

WHAT ARE GRASSLAND FOOD CHAINS LIKE AROUND THE WORLD?

Every grassland is home to grasses, **primary consumers** that eat grasses and seeds, and hunting animals. But different grasses grow in each grassland **habitat**. These different grasses attract different animals. Temperature and rainfall also affect which plants, animals, and **decomposers** live in a habitat.

SERENGETI

The **Serengeti** is Africa's most famous **savanna**. This rolling grassland stretches across Tanzania and Kenya. A mix of grasses called sward attracts huge herds of **grazers**. Wildebeest, zebras, and other **herbivores** follow seasonal rains. Giraffes reach for acacia leaves. **Secondary consumers**, such as hyenas and lions, hunt the grazers. Five kinds of vultures live here, feeding on dead animals. Much of the land in the Serengeti is protected. But animals are still threatened by **poaching**, disease, **overgrazing**, and droughts.

This food web shows the ways **producers**, **consumers**, and decomposers are linked in a Serengeti food web.

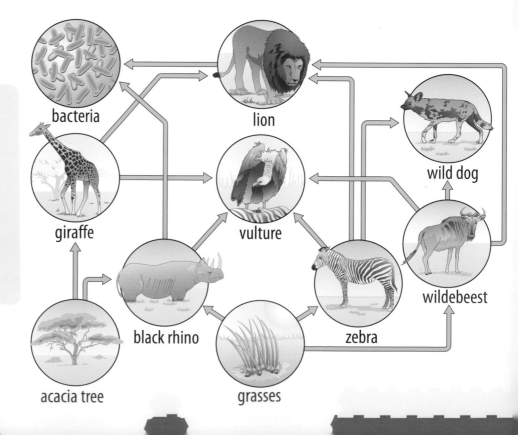

bacteria

lion

giraffe

wild dog

vulture

black rhino

grasses

zebra

wildebeest

acacia tree

HIGHVELD

Thick grasses and flowering plants once covered the high **plateau** of South Africa, called the Highveld. Farmers now grow corn, potatoes, and cattle on the land.

Only a few small nature reserves protect the Highveld. In the warm, wet summers, bunchgrasses and wildflowers grow. Winters are cold and dry. **Endangered** mountain zebras **graze** in the highveld, along with duikers and impala. Brown hyenas and leopards stalk the grazers. Peregrine falcons and fish eagles hunt from above. Nile crocodiles hunt in rivers that meander across the plateau.

White rhinos are not actually white. The name comes from a mistranslation of the word "wide," which was used to describe their mouths.

LOSING A LINK: WHITE RHINO

Herds of black wildebeest and white rhino once roamed the Highveld. These animals need large areas of grassland to survive. Much of the Highveld has been cleared for farming, cities, and mining. Because of habitat loss and hunting, the herds are disappearing.

AUSTRALIAN SAVANNA

Northern Australia has the largest remaining savanna in the world. It stretches over 1 million square kilometers (600,000 square miles).

This savanna is home to plants and animals that live nowhere else. Low, rolling hills are covered with grasses. Eucalyptus trees, cypress pines, and hardy shrubs grow among the grasses. Red kangaroos and emus graze here. Flying foxes feed on **nectar** and fruit. Frilled lizards catch ants and other insects and lizards.

After the hot, rainy summer, lush grasses dry and become fuel for fires. For thousands of years, **Aboriginal** people set small fires each year to keep areas open for hunting. Today, few people live in the northern savannas. As a result, dead grass litters the ground. Then large wildfires erupt, killing plants and animals. These fires also threaten towns and cities.

This food web shows the many ways **energy** is transferred in the Australian savanna.

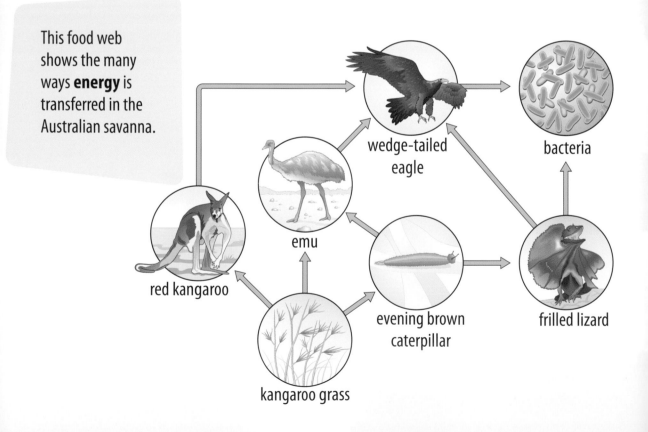

wedge-tailed eagle

bacteria

emu

red kangaroo

evening brown caterpillar

frilled lizard

kangaroo grass

Large herds of up to 8,000 Mongolian gazelle migrate together in the spring. They travel 200 to 300 kilometers (120 to 180 miles) a day.

EURASIAN STEPPE

The **steppe** of **Eurasia** stretches from Hungary to Mongolia, about 5,000 miles (8,000 kilometers). "Steppe" is a Russian word meaning "grassy plain." Less rain falls on this grassy plain than on a **prairie**, so shorter grasses grow.

The largest **temperate** grassland remaining in the world is the Mongolian steppe. Over one million Mongolian gazelles, called zeer, live here. They **migrate** across the steppe to find grass and onions. Wolves and steppe eagles hunt Mongolian gazelles. Severe snowstorms also kill many gazelles.

For thousands of years, herders grazed livestock on the steppe. They moved sheep, goats, and cattle from one area to another, so that the land was not overgrazed. Today, more land is farmed, and overgrazing threatens the steppe.

NORTH AMERICAN PRAIRIE

Prairie once covered the middle of North America, from Canada to Texas. Today, most of that land is now farmland or towns and cities.

In a prairie, tall bluestem grass reaches over the heads of bison. Colorful wildflowers attract butterflies, bees, and other insects. Bison, elk, and deer graze here. Prairie dogs dig mazes of tunnels underground and come to the surface to eat grass and seeds. Meadowlarks, bobolinks, and sparrows find insects and seeds. Rattlesnakes, coyotes, and hawks are secondary consumers here.

Fire, drought, and grazing animals keep trees from growing on prairies. Snow covers the prairie in winter. Green leaves and stems wither. Plant roots stay alive underground, and shoots regrow in spring.

Organisms in prairies make up a complex food web.

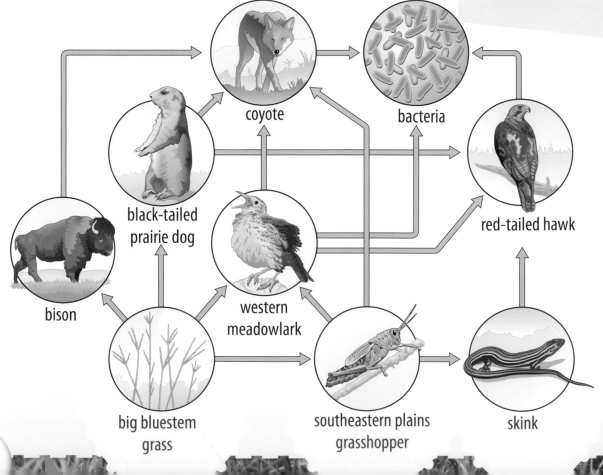

coyote

bacteria

black-tailed prairie dog

red-tailed hawk

bison

western meadowlark

big bluestem grass

southeastern plains grasshopper

skink

HUMID PAMPAS

The Humid **Pampas** was once a sea of grass stretching across Argentina. Some of the best grazing lands in the world are here. Farms, ranches, and cities now cover most of the Humid Pampas. Little natural **habitat** remains today.

Slow-moving rivers flow through the Humid Pampas. Feather grass, pampas grass, and other tall grasses cover these flatlands. Cattails, water lilies, and reeds grow in marshes in the pampas. Summers are hot and humid, while winters are cool.

At night pampas deer graze on plants. During the day, deer rest, hidden by towering grasses. Because much of the pampas habitat has been lost, the population of deer has declined. Hunting, poaching, and diseases have also taken a toll. Cougars are the deer's only natural **predator**.

Pampas foxes hunt in the cover of tall grass. A pampas fox catches birds, rodents, rabbits, frogs, and lizards.

HOW ARE HUMANS HARMING GRASSLAND FOOD CHAINS?

Grasslands cover about 25 percent of Earth's land. Their rich soils and flat landscape make them ideal for farming. For thousands of years, people lived and farmed grasslands with little impact on them. But modern farmers clear huge areas of grasslands to grow crops. Instead of leaving grasslands as **pastures** (land for **grazing**), some farmers clear the land and grow corn on it to feed cattle. In other places, domestic animals **overgraze** and harm grasslands.

Cities have also grown where there were once grasslands. Houses, schools, and factories have replaced large tracts of grassland. Every year fewer and fewer **native** grasslands remain. Around the world, grassland food chains are disappearing.

Farmers harvest wheat on fields where native grasses once grew.

Grasslands filter out pollutants from water.

PEOPLE NEED GRASSLANDS

Grasslands are home to plants that feed most people on Earth. Wheat, rice, and corn all began as grassland plants. People also have made medicines from grassland plants. If grassland plants and animals are lost, we will never know what new sources of food or medicine were possible.

Native grasslands also feed many of the animals that people depend on for food and clothing. Sheep, cattle, goats, and other domestic animals graze on grasslands around the world.

Grasslands help preserve the environment. When water seeps through grassland soils, some harmful chemicals are filtered out. The water is cleaned and safer for people to drink. Grassland plants also hold soil during rainy periods. Without these roots, soil **erodes** and washes into rivers and streams. Grassland soils help the environment by storing carbon, a chemical that can lead to **global warming** when it enters the **atmosphere**. When grasslands are farmed, their soils lose their carbon to the atmosphere.

A maned wolf hunts on the Cerrado.

HABITAT LOSS

The greatest threat to plants, animals, and **decomposers** in grassland food chains is **habitat** loss. A habitat provides grassland plants and animals with **nutrients**, water, sunlight, and shelter. When farms or cities take over grasslands, plants and animals lose their homes. If too much land is changed, many become **endangered** or go **extinct**.

Huge **prairies** covered the central United States before Europeans settled there. Very little natural grassland exists there today. About 20 percent of shortgrass prairies and 25 percent of mixed grass prairies remain. Only 1 percent of the original tallgrass prairies remain.

The Cerrado is the largest **savanna** region in South America. It covers southern Brazil and parts of Paraguay and Bolivia. It is home to more plants and animals than any other savanna. About 10,000 kinds of plants grow there. Almost half of these plants grow nowhere else in the world. People have changed more than 60 percent of the Cerrado. Farms, ranches, highways, cities, and roads threaten plants and animals in the Cerrado. Less than 2 percent of the Cerrado is protected.

CONTROLLING FIRES

Although you should never set a fire in a grassland, fire does help keep grasslands healthy. When a fire burns a grassland, plants regrow from their roots. The ash from a fire improves the soil.

People have tried to stop fires on grasslands. Without regular fires, the plant community changes. Shrubs and trees take root. **Nonnative** grasses that cannot survive fire become more common. As plants die each year, they litter the ground. This makes more fuel for a fire. When fire finally erupts, it is so hot that it damages native plants. As the plants change, grazing animals and their **predators** decline.

Fires help keep grasslands healthy.

ALIEN INVASION

Alien plants or animals can change a habitat. Some aliens are brought to new places on purpose for food, work, or gardens. Sometimes **species** are accidentally carried into habitats. Insects can hitch a ride on other animals. Seeds drop on cargo and get moved. In their new homes, alien species can grow out of control. They do not have natural predators or diseases. They use up limited water, space, and food. Native grassland plants and animals have trouble surviving when alien invaders change their habitat.

The cane toad is native to grasslands in Central and South America. This huge toad eats beetles that attack sugar cane plants. It also eats rodents, lizards, dog food, and human garbage. People brought cane toads to new places to control sugar cane pests. In their native habitat, many animals hunt cane toads. But in Australia nothing hunted the toad. Cane toads spread quickly across savannas and other areas. At water holes they devour lizards, insects, and insect-eating birds. Animals that try to eat them die from the toad's poison glands. What do you think would happen if another species like this were added to a grassland?

Cane toads have spread across savannas, devouring insects and lizards.

Global warming may threaten many grassland birds like this meadowlark.

CLIMATE CHANGE

Temperatures around the globe have risen in the past 100 years. This is called global warming. It is likely temperatures will continue to rise in grasslands. Scientists are not certain how this will affect grassland plants. In some areas, grasslands might face higher summer temperatures and more droughts. In other places, grasses could die early in the growing season. That would leave more moisture in the soil for trees and other plants.

Grassland animals will also be affected. For example, grassland birds may move north during nesting season to find cooler **climates**. But if the plants they eat do not spread to the same areas, then birds will find less food.

WHAT CAN YOU DO TO PROTECT GRASSLAND FOOD CHAINS?

Grasslands across the globe are disappearing quickly. The grasslands that remain are home to a rich variety of plants and animals. They include **endangered** plants and animals that live nowhere else on Earth. **Conservation** groups are trying to protect remaining grasslands.

LEARNING ABOUT GRASSLANDS

Scientists study the impact of fire, **grazing**, and **climate** on grasslands. Through their research, they learn how to best preserve grasslands and the animals that live in them.

At the Konza **Prairie** Biological Station in Kansas, scientists study how bison affect prairie plants. Millions of bison once roamed the North American prairies. By 1886 settlers had killed all the bison in Kansas.

In 1987, 30 bison were brought to Konza Prairie. Today, the herd has grown to 285 bison. Researchers have learned that more kinds of plants grow where bison graze than where cattle graze. Bison do not **overgraze** or harm prairie plants.

The Konza Prairie in Kansas preserves part of the tall grass prairie that used to cover much of the Great Plains.

The Indian government hopes to reintroduce the cheetah to Indian **savannas**.

BRINGING BACK A PREDATOR

Asian cheetahs once roamed on grasslands in India and the Middle East. **Habitat** loss and hunting led to the cheetah's extinction in India. The last time a cheetah was reportedly seen in India was 1968. Only a few cheetahs remain in Iran.

Now the Indian government wants to return cheetahs to its grasslands. It plans to bring in cheetahs from Africa. Cheetahs need large grasslands with plenty of **prey**. Some people worry that not enough grassland will be restored for the project to succeed. They think that the cheetahs will end up in open-air zoos instead of in the wild. Others think that returning cheetahs to India is a good idea. If the project succeeds, other endangered plants and animals will be protected. The grassland habitat will be conserved.

Ecotourism brings jobs and money to people who live near parks that preserve grasslands, such as this one that features grazing elephants.

ECOTOURISM

How can people earn a living and still preserve land? One way is to bring tourists to nature instead of developing the land. Manas National Park in Assam, India, has been a protected area for 100 years. The British government banned the hunting and killing of wildlife there. But **poaching** and smuggling of animals such as rhinoceros, tigers, and elephants still took place.

Now Manas National Park is an **ecotourism** site, a place where tourists can visit without harming the environment. Some people who once poached wildlife now work as guards. They teach their neighbors about the importance of conservation. They promote ecotourism to make more money for the park, conservation, and education.

KIDS IN ACTION

Eight-year-old Erik Uebelacker learned that butterflies taste with their feet and wanted to write about it. With his mother's help, he wrote a book titled *Butterflies Shouldn't Wear Shoes*. At first it was a gift for his teachers, but he soon began selling more copies. Erik gave the World Wildlife Fund $2,000 from the sale of his book. This organization protects grasslands and other habitats.

Butterflies also inspired eight-year-old Benjamin Workinger. Benjamin learned that monarch butterflies are in trouble during their migration. Monarch butterflies **migrate** 4,500 kilometers (2,800 miles) each year from Canada to Mexico and back. Along the way they must find milkweed plants for their caterpillars to eat. They also need flowers with **nectar**. The butterflies are finding fewer plants along their route.

Benjamin and his classmates decided to help. They planted a monarch garden at their school. Their garden has swamp milkweed, mammoth dill, wild indigo, giant coneflower, and Carolina pea. Their garden attracts monarchs, other butterflies, and birds.

A monarch butterfly colony surrounds children as they walk along a trail in Texas.

TOP 10 THINGS YOU CAN DO TO PROTECT GRASSLANDS

There are lots of things you can do to protect grassland food chains. Here is a list of the top 10:

1 Learn about grassland plants and animals and share your knowledge with others. The more people know about grasslands, the more they will want to conserve them.

2 Plant **native** grasses and flowers in your garden at home. Native plants attract native insects and other animals. They also need less water.

3 Clean your boots when you hike in a new area. Make sure that **alien** weed seeds do not hitch a ride on your boots.

4 Find out about local groups that restore grassland and other native **habitats**. Volunteer to pick up litter from a preserve or pull weeds of alien plants.

5 Write to an organization such as the Grassland Foundation and thank it for its work to preserve grasslands.

6 Set up a compost pile and use compost when you plant your garden. Compost helps improve the soil and reduces the need for pesticides and fertilizer, which can harm the environment.

7 Organize your class to plant native grasses and wildflowers in your schoolyard. Ask if you can change a mowed lawn into a grassland or other native habitat.

8 Ride a bike or walk to a friend's house instead of asking for a ride. You will save gasoline and help reduce **global warming**.

9 Help scientists monitor bird populations. Participate in local bird counts. Report your bird counts to online bird checklists.

10 Write to local and national officials, telling them that you support conserving grasslands.

GLOSSARY

Aboriginal having to do with the native people of Australia

adapted changes to a species that helps it survive

alien animal or plant that is brought by people to a new environment

atmosphere mass of air and gas that surrounds Earth

bacteria microscopic decomposers that live everywhere

bird of prey bird that hunts and kills other animals

carcass dead body of an animal

carnivore animal that eats other animals

climate weather conditions in an area

conservation protecting and saving the natural environment

consumer organism that eats other organisms

decomposer organism that breaks down dead plants, animals, and their waste to get energy and nutrients

ecotourism form of tourism focused on preserving the environment

endangered in danger of extinction (dying out)

energy power needed to grow, move, and live

enzyme chemical that breaks down compounds

eroding wearing away of rocks and soil by wind, water, ice, or chemicals

Eurasia the landmass that contains the continents of Asia and Europe

evaporate lose liquid to the air as water vapor

evolve to change over time

extinct no longer in existence (died out)

fungi group of decomposers that includes yeast, molds, mushrooms, and their relatives

global warming worldwide increase in air and ocean temperature

graze eat grass and other green plants in a field or meadow

grazer large mammals that eat grasses. Sheep, cattle, zebras, and antelopes are grazers.

habitat place where an organism lives

herbivore animal that eats only plants

larvae young stage of insects and other animals that does not resemble an adult

mammal warm-blooded animal that produces milk to feed its young

migrate to move from one area to another

native plant or animal that lives in the place where it evolved

nectar sugary substance made by plants

nonnative plant or animal that lives in an area where it was not born, grown, or produced

northern hemisphere the northern half of Earth

GLOSSARY

nutrient chemical that plants and animals need to live

organism living thing

overgrazing destroying plants by eating them down to the roots and trampling them

pampas grassy plains of Argentina

pasture grassy area used for grazing animals

photosynthesis process by which plants change energy from the Sun into food energy

plateau area of land that is raised above its surrounding area

poach to illegally hunt an animal

pollen small grains that are the male part of a flower. Pollen combines with the female part of a flower to form seeds.

pollinate fertilize a plant by transferring pollen from another plant

prairie temperate grassland of North America

predator animal that hunts and eats other animals

prey animal that is eaten by another animal; also, when an animal pursues another animal to eat it

primary consumer animal that eats plants

producer organism that can make its own food, using energy from the Sun

rhizome underground horizontal plant stem that produces shoots above and roots below

savanna tropical grassland with scattered trees

scavenger organism that feeds on dead plants, animals, and their waste

secondary consumer animal that eats other animals

Serengeti African savanna that is home to many grazing animals

species type of plant or animal

spore cell that grows into a new individual

steppe dry, temperate grassland

stolon horizontal stem above ground that produces new shoots

symbiotic system in which two organisms live together and both benefit

taproot main root of a plant that grows straight down from the stem

temperate region between the tropics and the polar circles

tropical region on either side of the equator

tuber underground stem or root that stores food

veld high grassland in South Africa

FIND OUT MORE

BOOKS

Aronin, Miriam. *The Prairie Dog's Town: A Perfect Hideaway*. New York: Bearport, 2010.

Davis, Barbara J. *Biomes and Ecosystems* (*Earth Science*). Milwaukee: Gareth Stevens, 2007.

Jackson, Kay. *Explore the Grasslands* (*Fact Finders*). North Mankato, Minn.: Capstone, 2007.

MacAulay, Kelley, and Bobbie Kalman. *A Grassland Habitat* (*Introducing Habitats*). New York: Crabtree, 2007.

WEBSITES

www.blackfootedferret.org/how-to-help.htm
Discover how to help black-footed ferrets and other endangered grassland animals.

www.butterfliesshouldntwearshoes.com
Learn how an eight-year-old boy wrote a book about butterflies and raised money for the World Wildlife Fund, which protects habitats around the world.

www.serengeti.org
Visit the animals of the Serengeti.

www.konza.ksu.edu/keep/
Go on a prairie science adventure.

www.actionfornature.org/eco-hero/ecoheroawards.html
Read about young people who have helped the environment and earned the Action for Nature International Young Eco-Hero Awards.

FURTHER RESEARCH

Choose a topic from this book you'd like to research further. Do you live near a grassland you would like to know more about? Or is there a faraway grassland you think is exotic? Was there a creature in this book you find interesting? Is there something harming grassland food chains you'd like to know more about putting a stop to? Visit your local library to find out more information.

INDEX